FREEDOM THROUGH SPORTS BETTING

MARIUS SMIT

Contents

KICK-OFF

Why this book?

Sports betting is in essence a wealth transfer from the masses to the few. The fuel for this process is information asymmetry. Stated plainly it is a lack of knowledge on the part of the average better, which is perpetuating this wealth transfer. This book takes no moral stance on sports betting or its participants. It does, however, aim to make the playing field of sports betting more even. It does so by providing anyone who is willing to learn with the knowledge needed to exit the state of perpetual losing. It is a guide for anyone who is serious about advancing on the road to successful sports betting. This is said in full awareness of how diverse the sports betting markets for the different sport disciplines are. It is also clear that no two readers will be at the same stage of development with regard to their sports betting skill set.

This book is the result of my own journey to profitable sports betting. It is the culmination of experience gained in more than a decade. It includes essential knowledge ranging from a winning mind-set to technical details, which are required for success. It targets both the novice and the seasoned sports better.

Although sport disciplines vary in many ways, from a sports betting perspective the fundamentals are the same. Regardless of the sport discipline, be it horse racing, football or baseball, in all cases, odds are calculated for the different outcomes and offered to betters before the event. What differs are the metrics used to calculate the odds. Throughout this book association football, or soccer, probably the most universal of sport disciplines, is used to illustrate the fundamental principles. These principles apply to all fixed-odds sports betting markets.

This book focuses on fixed-odds sports betting, the most common form of betting across sport disciplines. Fixed-odds betting simply means that the price, or pay-out, is fixed at the time the bet is placed. It is worth mentioning another method of betting employed for horse racing in some countries, called pari-mutuel betting. In this form of betting, the pool of bets (minus taxes and the so-called "vic", or charge) gets distributed amongst all winners. Hence, the pay-out is only fixed after the bet has been sold.

Every one of us has experience of learning something the hard way. Like me, you might have spent time doing something over and over again without getting markedly better at it. Hitting thousands of golf balls does not guarantee a person any progress at that beautiful game. Similarly, any number of bets you may place with the best intentions does not in itself bring you one step closer to being successful at sports betting. People who are good at something, good enough to be consistent winners at it, get to that level in large part because they call on the help of experts or professionals in order to develop their abilities.

Commitment is an important ingredient for success, but to go to the next level it is important to study the methods and call on the experience of winners. It should be obvious that sports betting is no exception. What sets it apart, however, from most other disciplines is the almost complete absence of professional role models. There simply are not many winners. Furthermore, this small group of successful sports betters, as opposed to golf professionals, to name only one example, are reluctant to tell their story and share their expertise. This book is a deliberate exception in this regard.

There are many obstacles you have to overcome in order to become a perpetual winner, betting on sports. Every one of those hurdles eliminates a percentage of individuals, who will simply never advance past that hurdle and will therefore remain perpetual losers. In many cases, this will sadly not be due to lack of ability, but due to failure to recognize the question which needs to be asked with regard to the hurdle that needs to be overcome. You can only find the answer if you ask the right question. This book will guide you to the main questions and provide proven answers.

Epiphany

I can vividly recall the days and weeks around the time that it happened. After twelve years of sports betting and having lost much hard-earned money, I had set out to find a way to beat the bookmaker permanently two years earlier. What followed was an intense period during which I focused all my faculties and resources on this mission. The time that I did not invest in my work as a systems analyst was spent almost exclusively on developing new ideas for a system that would give me an edge over the bookmaker.

I had decided to focus on football, or soccer, betting. I soon realized that a winning system would have to be based on reliable historical data. Fortunately, I found an internet site which provided detailed match data of the major European football leagues. Importantly the data set also included the odds of several major bookmakers for every one of those matches. The data was updated on a weekly basis and covered more than a decade of football matches. This data source turned out to be a treasure trove.

I was obsessed with making the data tell me where the bookmaker was vulnerable. My underlying assumption was that the bookmaker could not or would not always put out fair odds. The objective was to find an approach which would enable me to consistently identify those occurrences when the odds were not fair or accurate. This means the odds would not reflect the actual probabilities of the outcomes of a game. The search was a fascinating process.

First, I had to develop a method by which to determine the probability of the outcome of matches with at least the same amount of accuracy as the bookmaker. For months I experimented with a wide range of methods made possible by the rich data set which I had available. The core metrics I ended up applying included aspects like the relative offensive and defensive strength of each team during the season. These and other metrics contributed to the ranking of each team and were updated after each game. Based on historical data I developed a regression formula for each of the most prominent football leagues in Europe. This formula translated the ranking of two teams involved in a matchup into probabilities and therefore odds for the three possible outcomes of a game.

The second step was to validate this method against thousands of historical matches, with the objective of comparing the accuracy of the odds I had determined with those of the bookmakers. I managed to automate this process in a spreadsheet after having spent months on restructuring the data in order to automate the testing. This whole process was as consuming as it was fascinating, and continued for more than a year.

And then it happened. Having analysed countless methods, which I would compare to knocking on countless doors, one had suddenly sprung open. The simulations showed isolated but systemic weaknesses in the bookmakers' odds, with varying degrees in the different leagues. I validated the results several times, and then I knew with certainty that I had found a method to make a modest, but sustainable, profit on football betting. The realization that I could have an income from something I intensely enjoyed was liberating.

There was still much to learn, especially with regard to money management and the response of bookmakers to a winning customer. Importantly though, I had found the key that I was looking for. In finding this winning formula, I had crossed the divide from the losers to the winners. This is a thin line that separates these two states of human experience. This line is, to the masses, an insurmountable hurdle and, to the privileged minority, a point of no return. It determines whether a person is scraping through, or has access to vast resources. What took me across this line was an obsession with sports betting and the commitment to do whatever it takes to be a winner at it. With this book, I aim to give one person a hand across that line. I hope that person is you. Let us get started.

REASONS WHY LOSERS LOSE

Mismatch

Placing bets on future events is an integral part of human economic behaviour. Any and every action involving the exchange of one asset for another with the intent of making a profit from this action is at its core a bet. Whenever the estimated probability of a future outcome can be determined fairly accurately, and the potential return involved more than compensates for the risk, such an action is commonly referred to as an investment rather than a bet. For now, we will stick with the term bet.

A bet is a transaction between two parties. For the sake of convenience, and to minimize transactional costs, market places exist to bring together the parties to a bet. For bets on future sport events the probability of an outcome is translated into a price, expressed as odds. As in any market place the ability to consistently determine accurate odds of future outcomes is the key element which determines the success or failure of a participant in the sports betting market. Bookmakers are very good at calculating odds; the betting public at large, much less so. Unfortunately, for the vast majority of sports betters this translates into losses.

While the majority of betters consistently lose vast amounts of money in total, a relatively small group of individuals are profiting handsomely. Put simply, there are two groups of participants in the sports betting market place. There are the perpetual winners and the perpetual losers. The winners are the bookmakers and a very small percentage of the betters, also called sharps. This group approaches every betting market in a rational and calculated way. Calculated in this sense is also meant literally. Bets are only offered or accepted when, in the calculation of the bookmaker or sharp, the actual probability of the outcome is not correctly reflected in the odds. Hence, the odds represent value, meaning the relationship between risk and reward is favourable.

To determine whether the underlying odds offer value bookmakers and sharps process vast amounts of information in a highly effective way. This is done computerized with statistical analysis of very detailed databases of historical sport events. In addition, information from insiders is gathered and processed. If relevant, weather forecasts are analysed in order to determine any possible influence on the outcome of the event, hence on the odds. Bookmakers and sharps come to the sports betting market place well prepared. Hence, they win.

The second group, the perpetual losers, come to the market place in great numbers, bringing with them their hard-earned cash. They tend to behave emotionally, often experiencing emotional highs and lows during the betting process. It is quite simply a mismatch, played out millions of times every week. If you are a winning better, you will know this fact beyond any doubt, and you will have the winning record to back it up. If not, you are currently a loser. Squarely facing up to this fact is the first and vital step to breaking out of this group.

Process of losing

A few months after I had found my winning formula for football betting I opened an account with a very well-known United Kingdom based bookmaker, Ladbrokes. Although Ladbrokes generally offer terrible value, it was offering top odds on some of the markets that I was interested in. I therefore opened an online account with a fairly sizeable deposit. In the following three weeks, I placed seven bets on this Ladbrokes account. On balance, I was down 60 percent on my initial deposit as a result of these seven bets. Both to my surprise and subsequent delight, I received an email from Ladbrokes informing me that no further bets from me would be accepted.

The risk management team at Ladbrokes had needed only seven bets to determine that I had isolated vulnerable areas in their odds, and that I would inevitably become a non-profitable account from their perspective. There was not the usual reduction in my betting limits, it was simply too obvious. I did not need the confirmation from Ladbrokes that my formula was sound, but I did appreciate it anyway.

The important point that should be made here is that the risk management team at Ladbrokes is obviously very good at telling winners and losers apart. And this is critical to their long term success. In fact, any successful bookmaker has to be able to distinguish between winning and losing accounts by assessing betting patterns. Similarly, any conscious better has to be able to tell winning and losing patterns apart. Identifying losing patterns and recognizing their existence are the first steps towards ending them. In order to do so it is vital to understand the process of losing.

If the betting behaviour of losing betters has to be summed up in a single word, it has to be "emotional". Losing betters experience feelings of excitement, anticipation, anxiety and disappointment (and, less often, elation) in varying degrees at various stages of the betting process. These feelings are completely foreign to a winning better. Most losing betters, if not all, are motivated by hope. This might go much deeper than the mere hope of making a profit on sports betting. In my experience, the underlying motivation of a losing better is very often the hope of changing one's situation for the better on a more general level.

Going to work day after day to do something which is less than satisfying, and getting paid badly for it, is depressing. It is easy to understand that someone in such a situation would jump at the opportunity of making a bet in the hope of winning some easy money on the next sports event. Identifying and understanding what it is that you would like to change in your life through winning at sports betting is well worth looking at more closely.

As the better is driven to the act of betting by hope, the time immediately leading up to actually placing the bet is filled with anticipation and excitement. Placing a bet with the potential of winning money on an exciting sports event just a short time away can do to grown-ups what Christmas Eve does to a child. Unlike winning betters, losers often actually follow the event they placed a bet on as it is taking place. This frequently leads to a period of anxiety, due to the fear of losing. The perpetual losing better will naturally also experience winning bets, but the more regular feeling will be that of disappointment. Losing at sports betting can at times be a very lonely place. The combination of hard-earned cash having been lost and the realization that your own judgment let you down can be extremely disheartening.

Fortunately, the human mind has the ability to recover from disappointment. As other ideas flow into the realm of thinking, the numbness caused by the loss fades away. It does not take long for hope to flare up again, and the losing cycle is entered into once again. At best, the losing better can keep the process going without serious side effects in his personal situation. At worst, this process is a downward spiral with dire financial and personal consequences.

There is no such thing as luck in sports betting

Understanding the processes of losing and recognizing it in one's own behaviour is a vital step towards turning losing habits into winning habits. It is equally important to understand why the odds of winning are literally stacked against the better. Millions of people engage in sports betting in the hope of somehow adding something they otherwise lack to their personal situation. In doing so, they ironically rely on the one factor which is completely absent in the sphere of sports betting; luck.

Whether you are one of the millions who continuously lose money or one of the few who continuously profit depends primarily on your understanding and acceptance of the following truth. There is no such thing as luck involved in sports betting. You might sense an urge to resist this fundamental truth. You might also recollect situations which, in your opinion, clearly illustrate the cruel nature of luck in sports betting. Most sports betters can recall an event in which everything conspired against what should have been an obvious winning outcome, only for them to lose that bet through a stroke of "bad luck". Human beings have an impulse to believe in the existence of higher powers. Relying on the existence of some higher power or believing that one is subjected to the outcome of events, brought about by a factor like luck, are simply ways of delegating responsibility for one's actions and situation.

If something works out as planned, we gladly accept credit for having analysed the situation correctly and having acted sensibly. If something does not work out, we look for unknown factors that prevented our plan from being a success. The vaguer these factors are, the better, which is why bad luck is such a widely used alibi amongst sports betters. You can test this on yourself. Think of the number of times you won bets only through sheer good luck as opposed to the number of times you lost through sheer bad luck. It is very likely that you will recall more bets that you lost through what you call bad luck than you will recall bets you only won through good luck.

To illustrate this point better, let us construct an example. Imagine there is a group of people in your local community who take a very keen interest in birds. In fact, they are so passionate about birds that many years ago they formed an organization, which they called Birds365. They chose this name because they are literally occupied with birds every day of the year. Throughout the years they have studied every conceivable aspect of the biology and behaviour of birds. The group includes specialists from different areas of science to give Birds365 a unique insight into all matters surrounding birds. They keep records of bird migration patterns, the underlying weather conditions, feeding and mating patterns. Representatives of the group even travel to far away regions to which birds migrate during winter in order to better understand migration habits. The local council consults with the group frequently to ensure that infrastructure projects in no way influence bird population numbers. Analysing their records, the group can make very precise estimations of the exact migration behaviour and times, as well as future population numbers of the local bird types.

In order to entertain the local community and generate income for Birds365, members of the group offer bets on issues surrounding birds at the local pub. Bets are offered on things like the exact date on which the first bird of a type will appear after the spring migration, the number of offspring it will have, the number of weeks that will pass before the offspring arrive, the mortality rate, etc. Now let us imagine an individual at the local pub who regularly takes on the bets offered by Bet365. The person enjoys putting out some breadcrumbs for the pigeons in the local park, has often watched the pigeons scramble for the crumbs and has come to consider himself a bit of an "expert" on pigeons and birds in general. The person tends to lose more bets on bird matters than he wins. And now let us imagine this person regularly referring to himself as being unlucky for losing money on the bets he makes against Birds365. Would you not consider such an interpretation of "luck" as at least far-fetched? And yet, millions of sports betters do exactly the same when they look for the cause of their losses in the factor of luck.

Sports betting is a science. As in any science, there is no short cut to success. Without the proper knowledge and disciplined practice, profiting from it remains little more than a mirage of hope for the masses. In sports betting there are only winning or losing as long-term outcomes. There is no fence to sit on. Similarly, there are only two ways in which sports betting should be approached. It can be viewed as an entertaining way to ultimately lose money. Alternatively, it can be viewed as the science that it is. In this case you must accept the fact that luck plays no part in it and that you are solely responsible for success or failure.

Obstacles to Winning

The bookmaker juice

The one thing all bookmakers have in common is that they do make money over the long term. Where they vary greatly is how much money they make from each better and how they go about this. Let us first look at what they do. Bookmakers offer a convenience service for betters by offering a single point of contact. Imagine you had to go out and find somebody to take the other side of every bet that you want to place. This would be rather inconvenient. It is therefore only logical that the bookmaker should be rewarded for providing this service. The bookmaker collects this reward in the form of the so-called "juice".

The juice is a portion of the money placed on all the bets in a market which the bookmaker keeps, and therefore does not pay out to betters. How exactly is this done? Let us look at an example for a football betting market. The event is a game at Goodison Park between Everton and Liverpool in the English Premier League. There are three possible outcomes to the game, home win, draw, away win. The true probability calculated by the bookmaker of the outcomes expressed as percentages and odds could look like this.

Outcome	Percentage	Odds	
Home win	50%	2	(1/50*100)
Draw	30%	3.33	(1/30*100)
Away win	20%	5	(1/20*100)
Total	100%	1	(1/100*100)

Notice that the probability of all three outcomes together equals 100%, as one would expect. Now let us look at the way the bookmaker might make the odds available to the betting public.

Outcome	Percentage	Odds	
Home win	51%	1.95	(1/51*100)
Draw	32%	3.1	(1/32*100)
Away win	22%	4.5	(1/22*100)
Total	105%	0.95	(1/105*100)

Notice that the percentage for all three outcomes together now equals 105%. This means that the bookmaker keeps 5% juice and pays out only 95% of all the money taken in.

Taxation

Sports betting is simply too attractive for governments as a source of revenue to not be taxed. The way in which, in combination with the extent to which sports betting is taxed, in a country has a direct impact on the potential for a sports better to make a profit.

Generally, the two models for taxation that can be distinguished are taxation of the bookmakers' profits or taxation of the individual stakes. Countries with an established culture of sports betting and a moderate policy of taxing sports betting tend to opt for the first model. A 20 per cent rate of taxation on the bookmakers' profits could be typical. In such an environment the better is not directly confronted with the issue of taxation.

In the second model each bet placed is taxed at the time of the transaction. Under such a regime the better not only has to overcome the percentage of juice taken by the bookmaker, but also the percentage of tax taken by the state. To make things worse, in countries with this model bookmakers with high juice percentages tend to dominate.

Profitable sports betting in such an environment is practically impossible. A realistic edge over the bookmaker simply gets consumed by the tax. Positive expectation betting is not possible. Under these circumstances, it is difficult even to make a case for recreational betting. It is regrettable that profitable sports betting is not possible in many countries, but facing up to this reality and refraining from sports betting altogether is preferable to being ignorant or in denial.

Human thinking

The way you naturally think presents a huge obstacle to your potential to be a profitable sports better. The human brain is a product of the evolutionary process of millions of years. Throughout millennia it has been sculpted by the basic evolutionary purpose of survival. Some patterns of human thinking behaviour have been proven to be conducive to survival and as a result have been hard-coded into the human brain. These hard-coded thinking patterns are called heuristics and represent rules of thumb, which guide important aspects of human behaviour.

In a situation of sudden and imminent danger an individual will tend to follow the behaviour of other group members. Imagine a group of people sitting around a fire in the dark. If most of the group members suddenly jump up and scatter away in one direction a person who has otherwise not noticed anything will most likely also get up and run away. This is the result of the heuristic of social proof. Over millennia it has been proven to be prudent to follow the behaviour of the group. It is likely that a group will be able to take in more information than an individual member and, as a general rule of thumb, it serves the individual well to imitate the behaviour of the group.

Such intuitive behaviour has served humans well in their bid for survival throughout history. In modern day life the same behavioural patterns can, however, be detrimental to our success. Sports betting is most definitely an endeavour in which heuristics are detrimental to success. Human beings are in fact ill-equipped for successful sports betting. It is important to realize this, because only then can one eliminate erroneous hard-coded thinking which results in losing patterns.

Are we merely slaves to our hard-coded behavioural thinking or is there, in fact, a way to circumvent flawed thinking? A human being is capable of two kinds of cognitive processes, both of which will be referred to as thinking. The first kind is intuitive thinking which, for example, causes us to run away with the group in a situation of perceived danger.

The second kind of thinking is of a more deliberate nature. The process by which these thoughts come about takes longer, and information is gathered and processed in a more deliberate manner. Sports betters typically employ both kinds of thinking in their decision-making, for the most part to their disadvantage. Intuitive thinking, or heuristics, has served humans well in terms of survival over thousands of years; however, in sports betting this kind of thinking can be outright disastrous.

Here are some of the heuristics which cause flawed decision-making by sports betters.

Anchoring

The *Anchoring* heuristic describes the tendency in decision-making in which an individual is influenced by a prior piece of information, although that information may be incomplete or irrelevant to the question at hand. Take an example of two groups of people, each asked one of the following questions.

Group 1

What is the probability of Liverpool beating Everton in the next match if the stadium crowd is 75% male?

Group 2

What is the probability of Liverpool beating Everton in the next match if the stadium crowd is 50% male?

A variety of similar experiments have shown that group 1 will on average assign a higher estimated probability to a Liverpool win than group 2. This is done although the percentage of males in the crowd should have no bearing on the outcome. Any given number is taken as an anchor, although it is irrelevant to the question at hand. A plausible explanation for anchoring from an evolutionary perspective could be that, given complete uncertainty, the human mind is prepared to accept any initial point of reference.

In sports betting this heuristic, however, leads to flawed decision-making. Imagine a betting market with initial odds which do not reflect the true probability of the outcome by a substantial margin. The sports better will intuitively use these odds as an anchor and will be influenced by these initial odds as he follows the subsequent changes in the odds.

Availability bias

The *availability bias* heuristic is based on the very basic evolutionary notion that something is of importance if it can be remembered. As a result humans ascribe greater importance to recent events or dramatic events that leave a strong impression on the mind. Most football fans can recall a dramatic cup final between two prominent clubs. The impressions of that one game and its outcome will be in the back of the person's mind for many years as he assesses betting opportunities on subsequent meetings between the two clubs involved.

Representativeness

The representativeness heuristic refers to the belief that a small sample of events should follow the same characteristics as a large sample of events. An example of representativeness is the Monte Carlo Fallacy. The typical Roulette player tends to believe that after a sequence of spins in which only black came up the likelihood of red coming up increases. This is a fallacy, as the likelihood of red coming up remains exactly the same with every spin of the wheel.

There is, of course, the law of averages. However, this law applies for long sequences of events. *Representativeness* is the fallacious believe that, for example, after twenty spins in which black came up the law of averages should apply already, thereby increasing the likelihood of red coming up. In sports betting this heuristic leads to the temptation to back a team because *"they are due a win"*.

These are only three examples of heuristics which have served humans well in terms of survival, but which are certain to undermine the sports better who is not able to recognize their influences on his assessment of probabilities. Only a system which eliminates flawed intuitive thinking through a rational statistical approach can lead to success at sports betting. The development of such a system is the theme of the next chapters.

WINNING FUNDAMENTALS

Can you be a successful sports better?

Jesse Livermore was an infamous American stock trader who made and lost millions of dollars speculating on the stock market. Livermore was a keen student of mass psychology and personally experienced the stock market crashes of 1909 and 1929. In 1940, the year of his death, Livermore's book *How to Trade in Stocks* was published. These are the first sentences from it.

"The game of speculation is the most uniformly fascinating game in the world. But it is not a game for the stupid, the mentally lazy, the person of inferior emotional balance, or the get-rich-quick adventurer. They will die poor."

The vast majority of sports betters do get poorer, literally with every bet they place. The reasons they do so are those cited by Livermore. In order to become successful one's behaviour therefore has to change dramatically.

- Overcome mental laziness and engage in rational analysis
- Remove emotion completely from the whole process of sports betting
- Relinquish unrealistic short term profit expectations and approach sports betting as an investment with marginal potential for profits only over the long run

What exactly does each of these three changes in attitude and behaviour imply? It is essential to go into a more detailed analysis of what it takes to be successful, as the necessary skill set includes very specific attributes.

Sports betting is fundamentally an exercise in statistics. Statistics is a branch of mathematics and a process of collection, analysis and interpretation of data. In order to be successful at sports betting one therefore requires a basic understanding of statistics and the ability to conduct basic mathematical operations on data. The types of calculation required are best made using a computer program such as a spreadsheet application. Being able to use a spreadsheet program is a vital pre-requisite for success.

If one approaches and conducts sports betting as an exercise in statistics, as should be the case, the perils of emotions are avoided as a consequence. A sharp better will not watch or otherwise follow the underlying event of an active bet. There is no point in doing so. The bet is already placed on the basis of sound analysis, and the outcome will merely be one more result in a long sequence of results embedded into a winning formula which has been validated. Only a perpetual loser will place a bet on an event and then follow that event as it is unfolding, while going through a spectrum of emotions. A sharp better develops a winning formula, validates this formula thoroughly and then applies it in a disciplined manner. Sharps are not the flamboyant type. They are meticulous individuals who maintain realistic winning expectations. They understand that sports betting presents market places which are highly competitive, and that success is a result of superior skill and discipline.

There is one more attribute which is indispensable in the makeup of a successful sports better, money management. Without a sound concept of money management, no amount of skill or application of a winning formula will lead to success.

I would strongly encourage you to assess your mental attributes and skill set in a critical manner. Do you really possess the pre-requisites for success?

The cure for losing is winning

There was a time in my own development when I looked for any information I could get my hands on that would lead me closer to my goal of succeeding at sports betting. It turns out there are only a handful of quality books available. One of the books that were valuable to me was *Betting on Yourself* by Dr. Robert Anthony. As Dr. Anthony writes, *"When the student is ready, the teacher appears".* This turned out to apply to my situation at the time. In *Betting on Yourself* he writes that the most productive cure for losing betters, even problem gamblers, is for such a person to learn what it takes to become a winning better. This might sound like a very simplistic approach, but it is absolutely true and has been statistically proven. It furthermore truly reflects my personal experience.

To really understand something is to be liberated by it (Ross Ashcroft)

This theme, more than anything else, has been my motive to write this book. The aim is to assist you to fully grasp the fundamental truths about sports betting.

Chance, probability and odds

The chance of anyone who does not understand probability making a profit from sports betting is zero.

Sports betting is a game of chance. This is simply another way of saying that we can't know with certainty what outcome an event will have. One could, for example, say that for a given match team A has a good chance of beating team B. This is not a precise measurement of the likelihood of a win for team A. In order to determine the precise likelihood the probability has to be determined. Chance is a common, albeit not very precise, word for use in everyday life. Probability is a precise measure, which is calculated on a mathematical basis that can be expressed in percentages. For the purpose of betting, probabilities are converted into odds.

Odds can be expressed in different formats, which vary between countries. A coin toss has a probability of 50% of one side coming out top. A conversion into decimal odds will result in 2.00, whereas a conversion into fractional odds will result in 1/1 or evens.

The following table provides an overview of some probabilities in percentages expressed in different odds formats and locations.

Probability	Decimal	Fractional	US	Hong Kong	Indo	Malay
67%	1.50	1/2	-200	0.50	-2.00	0.50
50%	2.00	1/1	+100	1.00	1.00	1.00
40%	2.50	6/4	+150	1.50	1.50	-0.67
33%	3.00	2/1	+200	2.00	2.00	-0.50

The underlying basis for every bet is a probability of the outcome of an event. It is simply not good enough for a better to know that there is a good chance of a given outcome. It is vital that the better is able to determine the probability of an outcome precisely and to express this as a percentage. For this reason the chapter "Winning Systems" is dedicated to the development of systems that enable the sharp better to calculate probabilities in a reliable way.

Positive expectation betting

Most of us have a picture of a casino complex in our heads. For many people Las Vegas is such an image, but you might know a casino complex closer to home. Casinos are very often lavish centres with hundreds or even thousands or staff members. What most people do not realize is that casinos are extremely heavily taxed by the authorities. This is the main reason casinos are licensed to operate in most countries. It is quite simply incredibly profitable both for the owners and the government. Have you ever really taken the time to think where all this money is coming from?

Imagine you were given a licence to collect 1% of every unit of money spent at a supermarket chain in your country. At the checkout counter, before every payment 1% would be added to the amount and forwarded to your account. You would be doing well, and would be able to build lavish outlets. On the other side of the deal would be millions of customers, each of whom would be getting 0.99% (1/101*100) less value for their money. That is the business model of casinos in a nutshell. The casino games have an edge for the house which are built into the rules of the games. The edge ranges from about 1% for Blackjack, depending on the version of the game, to about 2.7% for single zero Roulette and 5.26% for double zero Roulette.

Many people do not recognize this fact clearly, because they might win some and then lose some. What they fail to recognize is that, in fact, statistically they are losing about a percentage of their money on every single bet. It does not matter how "good" a Blackjack player you are, every time the dealer lays the cards you have lost about 1% of your stake. You are literally being milked for your money. The trip to the casino is a losing proposition. Your winning expectation is always negative.

Throwing money at any game with a negative winning expectation is a delusional and irrational thing to do. This has to be realized fully. To stand any chance of being successful at betting it is vital to find betting opportunities with a positive expectation. A positive betting opportunity is when the odds offer value. Let us look at an example.

On the most widely used Roulette tables there are the numbers 0 – 36 (37 numbers). The house offers odds of 37/1 on any number, but it only pays out 36/1 on a winning number. Let us imagine the house were to make some changes and start offering different odds on different numbers. Let us say for numbers 0 – 18 it would pay 34/1 and for number 19 - 36 it would pay 38/1. You would calculate the true odds of every number to be 37/1. By placing your money on the numbers 19 – 36 you would have an expectation of a pay-out of 38/1. You would have a positive expectation. You would have found value. This is what is called positive expectation betting.

Unfortunately, it is unlikely that casinos are going to get into the business of positive expectation betting. The good news is that bookmakers are in this business. They might be very good at ensuring that they are on the positive side of the expectation divide, but in principle the better has the possibility of a positive expectation. Fixed-odds sports betting offers the opportunity for positive expectation betting. Hence, the focus of this book is on fixed-odds betting.

Bet selection

Fixed-odds sports betting provides an environment for the sharp better to make a profit over the long term. Still, sports betting markets are extremely competitive and a proven winning approach is necessary to be successful. The most vital aspect of a winning approach is bet selection. Which then, should be the determining factors for bet selection?

The goal of profitable betting can only be achieved if the better is able to find and maintain an edge. An edge is found when the better is able to identify bets for which the bookmakers' odds do not reflect the true probability of outcomes. The art of doing so is discussed in later sections. For now it is sufficient to understand that a better with an edge is able to identify and bet on odds which are more favourable to him than they should be. Such bets are known as value bets. The most critical attributes of a winning approach are that the better applies a system by which value bets can be reliably identified, and that he only wagers on value bets.

The majority of sports betters believe that profitable betting can be achieved by picking winners. This is a fallacy. While one would obviously have to win some bets in order to make a profit, the selection of bets should not be determined by the attempt to identify winners in the underlying event. This is very counter-intuitive and might well cause some resistance in you at this moment. It is possible to pick and land a winner and still be a loser.

Imagine going to the store to buy a product and paying 20% more for it than a fair price would have been. Once you have left the store with the product, will only the possession of the product be on your mind, or will you sense disappointment at having been overcharged 20%? Now imagine repeating this process of diminished returns for a sequence of purchases. Selecting winners as a method for identifying bets to wager on is like finding and buying products without checking the price in the process. A winning approach will not focus on picking winners, but on picking value.

A winning approach will, furthermore, be based on singles betting. That means that each bet will involve only one underlying event. Doubles, trebles and other multiples should be avoided. These bets on a number of underlying events offer no potential for positive expectation betting. This is not to say that individual bets within a multiple cannot hold value, but for the most part multiples serve the optimization of profit margins of the bookmakers and should at best be viewed as entertainment. It is comparable to playing the lottery and has no place in a serious approach to profitable betting.

Importance of historical data

Over a period of twenty years since my first exposure to sports betting I have learned many valuable lessons which have culminated in the ability to develop winning formulas. During that time I explored many, if not all, approaches to sports betting. The experience I gained has led me to the conclusion that success is only possible if sports betting is approached through the lens of statistical analysis. This might come as a disappointment to anyone who would rather believe that mere fixation with a given sport can be sufficient. Even watching thousands of hours of your favourite sport and reading any number of sports magazines a week will not bring success. Any strategy not based on sound statistical data analysis is a loser's game.

The underlying theme of statistical analysis in sports betting is that one can derive knowledge in the form of a winning formula from historical data and then apply such a system to make profits on future events. The premise for such an approach is the availability of a reliable historical data set for the specific sports betting market. Historical data is the treasure trove of the sharp better.

The process of finding an appropriate data set is a hurdle that every aspiring sports better has to take. The good news is that historical data sets are available on the internet for all of the most popular sports. The purpose of this section is to provide you with the knowledge needed to identify an appropriate data set and to structure the data for processing purposes.

An historical data set must include three characteristics.

- Statistics of the sporting events (matches, fights, races, etc.)
- Bookmakers odds and the time at which the odds were recorded
- Data for an extended historical period (e. g. several years)

It is impossible to know upfront which market to target for a given sport. That means to know where value is to be found. In fact, this is precisely the question which is addressed via the analysis of the data. For this reason it is preferable to utilize a data set which is as rich as possible when it comes to types of statistics. Any data point of the type of event which is captured consistently can prove to be of value in the search for an edge in a given market. In a data set for a football (soccer) league the following data points should ideally be included.

- Date of the match
- Home and away teams
- Number of home and away goals at half time and at full time
- Number of shots and shots on target
- Number of corners
- Number of yellow and red cards
- Odds for different markets like three-way and two-way match results and under and over number of goals for a number of well-known bookmakers

The purpose of data analysis is to determine patterns of value in the odds and extrapolate these patterns into the future. It is important to know the time at which the odds were recorded, as this aspect can be used in some systems. The bookmakers' odds might consistently be different on the evening before matches from match day, as the masses tend to place their bets on match day. It is therefore important to consider the time at which the odds were recorded.

The number of events or fixtures in a data set is critical with regard to its usability. The number of events included in a data set should be sufficient to allow a statistically significant analysis. Although this is a critical element of any system, it is not possible to specify here what particular number of events a data set has to include. Throughout this book football (soccer) is used for illustration purposes. The data set which is used for the major European leagues comprises nine consecutive seasons. Depending on the number of matches played during a season upward of 2500 matches per league are included in the data set. As a rough rule of thumb a data set should not include less than 1000 events in order to be statistically significant.

Data processing tools

In the previous section the importance of an historical data set which is sufficiently large was discussed. Manual processing of such a data set is impractical, if not impossible. A large number of calculations are necessary. In addition simulation runs will need to be conducted in order to validate potential formulas. It is therefore critical to select a computerized tool with which to process the data. A wide spectrum of solutions is available. Although the combination of a database and a programming language allows the most processing flexibility, it is only a solution for those with advanced programming skills. Fortunately extensive data analysis capabilities are also available to the average computer user.

Spreadsheet programs offer all the functionality which is needed to analyse historical data and develop a winning formula. Not every spreadsheet user is, however, familiar with macros. This is a function which allows the user to loop through a data set while doing calculations. This function can be used to answer a question like; what would the profit have been over the duration of a season if a specific betting formula had been used? Macros are very powerful, and yet easy to use.

It must be stressed that developing a winning formula for any sports betting market without computerized support is a futile exercise. For those who are not fortunate enough to possess such skills this might be a bitter pill to swallow. Not facing up to this reality, however, equates to getting into a bare fist fight with one's hands tied behind one's back.

Specialization

How does investing differ from betting? The most instructive distinction between a bet and an investment lies in the degree of certainty with which a positive return can be expected on the amount of money which is laid out. If one is able to make a reliable estimation of the probability of an outcome and find a bet on that outcome which is incorrectly priced to one's advantage, such a bet amounts to an investment. The determining factor is the degree of certainty with which a profit can be expected.

Certainty originates from deep rooted knowledge. Such knowledge is ultimately the result of specialization. Specialization is to drill down ever deeper into a given topic. In society, specialists are generally rewarded handsomely for their expertise. Similarly, in sports betting the masses pay while the specialist earns handsomely.

I once heard a story of a martial arts master who said;

I am not concerned about the opponent who has practised a thousand ways of striking me once, I am wary of the opponent who has practised one way of striking me, a thousand times.

Specialization is vital in order to be a successful sports better. Choose the sport you wish to bet on very carefully. Then choose the specific betting market for that sport, as carefully. And then zoom in on that market until you have confidence that no one person or bookmaker has drilled down deeper into all relevant aspects of that market. Even bookmakers with large teams can't study every market with an intense degree of detail. Apart from laying the platform for profitable investment, becoming such a specialist at a market is a very rewarding experience.

To be clear, being a specialist for a sports betting market does not mean you have to be a fan of the underlying sport. Although a thorough understanding of the sport is required, there is no need and little use in feeling passionate about the sport, having a favourite team or anything to that effect. Neither will excessive reading about the sport enhance your prospects of success. Only through statistical analysis of a sport and the corresponding betting market is profitable sports betting possible.

There are sports that are more suited than others for profitable sports betting. Some sports should be left alone altogether from a betting perspective. Sports that are played in a league format like Association football, or soccer, ice-hockey, baseball, basketball and American football offer the best opportunity for the sports better to gain an edge. Sports which are played in tournament format, including golf and tennis, do not provide the necessary data series continuity for reliable statistical analysis.

Becoming a successful sports better is a conscious decision. It is a decision to leave that sloppy losing feeling behind to instead approach sports betting as an investor does. It is a commitment to oneself to never place a bet unless it offers value determined on the basis of sound analysis. Specialization and a commitment to details is the foundation for sound analysis.

Winning systems

Value parameters

There is one fundamental truth which any sports better, if he is to become successful, has to fully comprehend and internalize.

A profit at sports betting will only be achieved over the long term if every bet on which a wager is placed is a value bet.

This truth is indisputable and therefore the main focus must be on identifying value bets. In order to determine whether a bet contains value one has to be able to compare the bookmakers' odds to the true odds according to one's own calculation. It is obvious that the quality and dependability of one's own calculation formula is paramount to success.

It is fair to assume that many betters' "calculation formula" might for example involve looking at the current form of a team, considering such things as the previous ten games, possible injuries, coaching changes and so on. Subsequently a decision is made as to the probable winner, a bookmaker is chosen and the stake is placed at the given odds. At no point in the process described above did the better have two sets of odds to compare, the bookmaker odds and the "true" odds. Any system employed to select value bets has to ultimately convert all the information taken into account into one's "true" odds.

Such a system can only be developed by learning from the past. In order to learn from the past about anything two aspects are vital, measurable parameters and repetition. We are able to learn from the past and recognize patterns if that which we are studying has parameters that we can measure and we can assess the influence of these parameters on the outcome via repetitions. Typical parameters include the number of shots on target in football, the number of punches landed in boxing or the number of home runs in baseball. These are all parameters which can be accurately measured, and their influence on the outcome of matches can be determined by studying repetitions.

To return to the example above, parameters such as injuries or changes in personal or weather conditions are nearly impossible to measure accurately, while only studying a repetition of ten matches would be too small a sample from which to make conclusions about the influence of these parameters on the outcome of games.

In a previous chapter the importance of a historical data set was discussed. It should now be clear that a historical data set which includes data on accurately measurable parameters and a sufficiently large number of repetitions or events is a vital pre-requisite for the development of a winning system.

Determining true odds

The aim of this section is to demonstrate how a system for determining the odds on the outcomes of events can be developed. A detailed study of a system which I developed over a period of months could easily fill a book. However, the focus is placed on the main steps in order to provide insight into the complexity and effectiveness of such a system without indulging in every detail.

The system which is illustrated is used to determine odds for the football three-way match betting market. At its core it is a ranking system with a distinction made between the home and away ranking for each team. The ranking is updated after every match day and is done on a season to season basis. This means that ranking values are calculated anew for every season and ranking values from the previous season are not taken into account. The first five season games of each team are discarded in order to allow for team performances to "settle".

A crucial aspect of any system is the underlying information set which is used. Generally a distinction can be made between quantifiable and non-quantifiable information. Quantifiable information is match data which includes everything from the number of goals, shots taken, shots on goals, corners, fouls, to the number of red cards. Non-quantifiable information includes, for example, specifics about the playing schedule, injuries to players, managerial changes and weather conditions.

The information set for this system is limited to quantifiable match data. The possible impact of a change of managers or weather conditions on a game is a science in itself, if not a philosophical issue. It lends itself in no way to support a system based on comparable data which produces statistically sound results. It is naïve to believe that one can gain an edge over the bookmaker based on such data. Not only is it is impossible to reliably translate such information into odds, but also the bookmaker should consistently have the data before the betting public does. Non-quantifiable information is best viewed as adding to the entertainment value of an event for the recreational better. It is not the stuff that winning systems are made of.

With the focus placed on quantifiable match data I had to decide how many past seasons to analyse and what factors would be the best indicators for the strength of a team. For all the major European football leagues data for nine previous seasons were available to me and so I decided to analyse six seasons, leaving three seasons with which to test the system. In terms of indicators for the strength of teams within the ranking the following three factors were chosen.

- ***Measure of domination*** over opponents or balance of play as measured by
  - Shots for / Shots against – the number of shots that the two teams had at goal is taken as an indicator for the balance of play
- ***Effectiveness of the offense*** as measured by
  - Goals for / Shots for – measures the quality of the offense in terms of converting opportunities into goals
- ***Effectiveness of the defense*** as measured by
  - Goals against / Shots against - this measure the quality of the defense including the goal keeper in terms of preventing the opposition from scoring

The next step involves calculating the values for these factors for each team for each match day. Then, the values for these three factors are added together into what is then the ranking value for a team. These values are calculated separately for home and away games, as teams are ranked in terms of both home and away strength.

In order to perform this retrospective calculation for every match day for six seasons efficiently the process has to be automated. I opted to do this by using the so-called macros functionality which is available in spreadsheet programs.

It is worth mentioning some variations to the parameters of the system, although an impact analysis of each of these variations proved to have no sufficiently positive effect to warrant inclusion.

- *"Smoothing" of extreme values. In particularly during the early part of the season some values like goals against in relation to shots against could distort the overall ranking.*
- *Calculated home and away ratings could be weighed with a factor for the relative strength of the opposition.*
- *The last n (example n = 5) number of matches could be weighed stronger than previous matches in order to accentuate the recent form of teams.*

At this point the system provides a ranking value for the home and away team before every match. For example; match day 34 of the Bundesliga season 2010/2011, Bayern Munich - Home 23.06 and Stuttgart Away 16.98. Although these values already provide an indication of the relative strength of the teams at this stage of the season they still can't be compared to the bookmakers' odds to determine whether value is available. In order to be able to do this these values first need to be translated into probabilities of a home or away win expressed in percentages.

The way to go about this is to take into account a large number of historical games and analyse what typically results were like when teams with similar rankings met. For this I used upwards of 2000 games per league, depending on the number of teams in a league and therefore the number of games per season.

The pivotal factor used is the difference in the rounded ranking values of the teams. In the example above of the game between Bayern Munich and Stuttgart the value for the pivotal factor is +6 (Bayern Munich Home 23 - Stuttgart Away 17 = +6). The historical data is used to determine what the percentage values for the three possible outcomes were for games in which the pivotal factor was +6. From the table below it can be derived that in 61 games in which the pivotal factor was +6 the outcomes were spread in the following way.

- home win 65% (rounded down slightly)
- draw 15%
- away win 20%

These values are now used as projected probabilities for a range of pivotal factors ranging from +10 to -10.

Pivotal factor	Games	Home win	Draw	Away win	Home win %	Draw %	Away win %
+10	17	13	3	1	76.47	17.65	5.88
+9	37	21	13	3	56.76	35.14	8.11
+8	37	24	10	3	64.86	27.03	8.11
+7	43	27	7	9	62.79	16.28	20.93
+6	61	40	9	12	65.57	14.75	19.67
+5	91	53	12	26	58.24	13.19	28.57
+4	108	63	28	17	58.33	25.93	15.74
+3	158	89	40	29	56.33	25.32	18.35

+2	189	90	55	44	47.62	29.10	23.28
+1	196	107	46	43	54.59	23.47	21.94
0	225	107	53	65	47.56	23.56	28.89
-1	180	78	50	52	43.33	27.78	28.89
-2	175	69	45	61	39.43	25.71	34.86
-3	142	50	42	50	35.21	29.58	35.21
-4	119	47	30	42	39.50	25.21	35.29
-5	100	28	27	45	28.00	27.00	45.00
-6	76	23	23	30	30.26	30.26	39.47
-7	66	21	15	30	31.82	22.73	45.45
-8	44	8	11	25	18.18	25.00	56.82
-9	32	9	7	16	28.13	21.88	50.00
-10	26	3	8	15	11.54	30.77	57.69

As can be seen in the example above, there are some irregular values in the percentages. For example, the value of 48% for home wins for the pivotal factor +2 is irregular considering that the values for +1 and +3 are 55% and 56% respectively. This is due to the number of historical games that are analysed. The greater the number of games used the more coherent these values would become.

We now have a system with which to statistically determine probabilities for the outcomes of games. By converting the percentage values into odds we are able to compare our odds with those of the bookmakers. For the example above it looks like this with odds for typical bookmakers taken a few hours before kick-off.

Bayern Munich – Stuttgart

If we take the probabilities we calculated above (home win 65%, draw 15%, away win 20%) we get to the following betting propositions.

	Home win	Draw	Away win
Our odds	**1.54** (1/65*100)	**6.67** (1/15*100)	**5** (1/20*100)
Bet365	1.29	5.5	10
Bet & Win	1.3	5.75	7.25
Lad-brokes	1.3	5.5	9
William Hill	1.3	5	10

According to our calculation the bookmakers' odds offer value on the away win. As it turned out, Bayern Munich won the game by 2 goals to 1. This is, however, only one match and according to the system a bet on Bayern Munich would have still been a losing bet as there was no value in the odds on the home win. This is assuming that the odds that were calculated were correct. This, however, still has to be validated.

For this purpose a general formula can be derived as a regression in order to make it possible to convert any ranking value to a percentage. This can be done by using the regression function of a spreadsheet program. The graphic below demonstrates how the equation can be derived for the calculation of home team probabilities for the German Bundesliga.

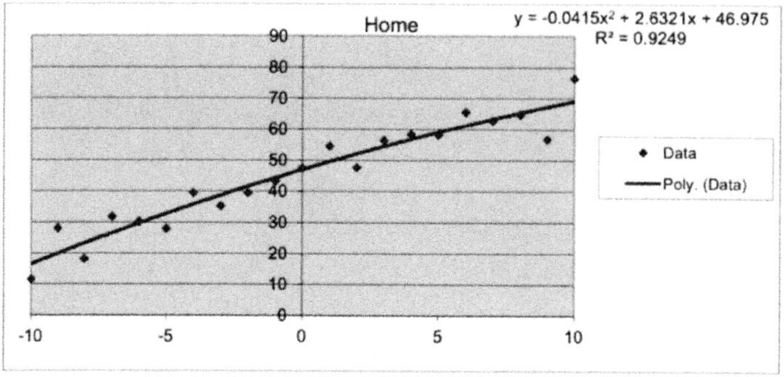

It is notable that with a coefficient of determination $R^2 = 0.9249$ a high correlation exists between the sample values.

Using the equation $Y = -00415x^2 + 2.6321x + 46.975$ the probability of a home win with a pivotal factor of $x = +6$ can now be calculated as 61.27% (odds 1.63).

In order to determine the quality of the system in terms of profits over the long term we now need to simulate what would have happened if this formula had been used for a given period. In order to do this we need to analyse a period which was not used for developing the formula. If the formula is used on the same data that was used to create it, the results would obviously be skewed. This is the reason why of the nine seasons of available data three seasons were left for testing purposes.

The simulation involves retrospectively calculating team rankings before every match day. Then converting the pivotal ranking values into probabilities of the home win, draw and away win using the regression equations created. Now the probabilities can be converted to odds and compared to the bookmakers' odds. If the bookmakers' odds offer value as compared to the calculated odds a bet is placed. Having completed the loop for all relevant match days during the three seasons it is now possible to assess the bankroll and put it in relation to the total staking amount to come to a conclusion about the profitability of the system.

The simulation can now be carried out using different settings. For example, the first five match days can be discarded as well as the last two in order to negate the impact of early season form issues and irregular results based on teams lacking motivation at the season-ending games while others may be highly motivated.

It should become obvious that such a statistical approach as is described here would not be suitable for tournament betting (e. g. UEFA World Cup), as suitable data sets would not be available. It should also be pointed out that the purpose of this chapter was to demonstrate how a formula can be developed based on statistical analysis. The results of this example should not be used for actual betting decisions.

Betting in a low-risk environment

The focus of the previous section was the development of a system by which true odds for future events can be determined through the statistical analysis of historical data. The underlying assumption that one can learn from the past and apply that knowledge to the future should be challenged by the astute better. In doing so one is likely to find a residue of doubt. This doubt should gain momentum when it comes to piling money into bets selected on the basis of such a system.

Ideally one should be able to use the possible benefits of such a system, but do so in a low-risk environment. That means one should be able to perform one's "magic" with the benefit of a "safety net". One should be able to exploit the possible upside benefits of the system and yet have little or no downside risk while doing so. Sound like a great idea?

Over the long term, through a combination of superior information and expertise, bookmakers are very good at determining accurate estimated probabilities for the outcome of sporting events. If there were a pattern of weaknesses in their odds it would be something that they would be aware of. There would have to be a reason for them to deliberately put out skewed odds. If a sharp better were equally aware of such a pattern of skewed odds he would be able to consistently profit from this knowledge. He would have found an edge from which to make profits.

This is the reason why Ladbrokes informed me that my account with them would be closed after just seven fairly sizeable bets. The risk management team at Ladbrokes obviously know very well where the weaknesses in their odds are and are diligently on the lookout for customers who, through their betting behaviour, prove that they also know these weaknesses.

Fortunately a small number of bookmakers (and betting exchanges) do not take positions on a betting market as the likes of Ladbrokes do, and act as a market maker, taking only a small percentage of juice for their service (e. g. Pinnacle). For these bookmakers the cornerstones of their strategy are betting volume and balancing their exposure across the possible outcomes to mitigate risk. Such a strategy allows them to permanently accommodate winning customers.

If one were able to identify a pattern for weaknesses in the bookmakers' odds it would be of great value if one could determine the extent of the weakness. It is, for example, conceivable that for a specific section in the complete range of odds in a market the odds could be so weak that one could make a profit simply by placing bets in that section of the odds. In order to illustrate how this would be possible it is helpful to construct a hypothetical scenario.

Let us assume that in a given European football league the odds on highly favoured home teams consistently hold value. The long term probability of a win for such teams could be 75% (true odds of 1.33). The bookmakers' odds over the same period could, however, reflect a home win probability of 73% (bookmakers' decimal odds of 1.37). Blindly placing bets on home team strong favourites would automatically guarantee profits as one would bet on average odds of 1.37 when the correct odds are in fact on average 1.33. This is obviously an example and by no means betting advice to blindly back home team strong favourites in European football leagues. The underlying principle should, however, be understood.

Staying with the hypothetical scenario, a strategy of betting on home team strong favourites would obviously hugely increase the potential for profits. On the other hand, and as a direct consequence, the odds on the underdogs hold negative value, and betting in this section would be very unwise.

It clearly makes sense to take the bets which are generated by one's own system and favour those that can be placed in a section of the market where the bookmakers' odds offer the best value generally.

The question now poses itself whether a low-risk betting environment actually exists. This question is the "holy grail" of sports betting. It is explored in the next section.

Identifying weaknesses in the bookmakers' odds

Now that the obvious benefits of exploiting weaknesses in the bookmakers' odds in certain sections of the market have been understood, the focus can shift to identifying such sections of weakness. In this section a systematic approach to determining weakness in bookmakers' odds will be illustrated for the football three-way fixed odds match betting market. The pre-requisite for such an analysis is once again a reliable and sizeable historical data set. The data set should comprise of match data for every match of the season for a number of seasons. To ensure that the sample data set used in the illustrated approach is statistically relevant, a period of five seasons will be used.

Although bookmakers seldom change their strategies for compiling odds and the amount of juice they extract completely, they do make adjustments. It is therefore important to analyse the odds of each bookmaker separately and for multiple seasons. Even some mainstream bookmakers have come under pressure from competitors with smaller margins and betting exchanges in recent years and, as a consequence, have changed their strategies by reducing their juice appreciably.

It might be sensible to not use all matches of a season. Leave out up to five match days at the beginning and two at the end of the season. The bookmakers also find it challenging to handicap early and season-ending games. Having considered this periodic aspect of the data set, the content of it now needs to be determined.

For the illustrated approach the data set includes the following facts for each match.

- Date
- Teams
- Result
- Odds for the relevant bookmaker

It is important to know at which approximate time the odds were recorded. Once weaknesses have been determined, the sharp can then analyse the odds at this time, and plays bets at this time. This aspect of time is vital. If, for example, weaknesses have been identified in odds recorded on the morning of match day, then the exploitation of these weaknesses should be done on the basis of odds as they stand on the morning of match day. The time factor could be an important component of the bookmakers' strategy. On the morning of match day, for example, the bookmaker wants to lure the masses in by offering skewed odds, for example by cutting odds on big name teams and extending odds on the away teams.

The first step is to arrange the data in such a way that it is possible to simulate the following scenario. What would have happened if every bet in a certain section of the market had been taken? The most basic three sections are odds on home win, draw or away win. The first step is therefore to simulate or reproduce what would have happened if one had blindly placed even stakes on every home team for the complete season and repeated the process for a number of seasons. For example, what would the result have been if one had placed an even stake bet on every home team during the English Premiership seasons from 2008/2009 through 2012/2013?

In the next step one would repeat this simulation with even stake bets on the draw and finally on the away teams. At this point it will be possible to make a first assessment. It will become apparent that the bookmakers' juice is higher on away team odds than on home team odds. To really sniff out weaknesses in the bookmakers' odds the next step is to assess more specific sections of the range of odds. For example, instead of placing an even stake bet on every home team one would only place that bet if the odds were between 1.5 and 2 (decimal) or probabilities of 66.67% (1/1.5*100) and 50% (1/2*100). Now it becomes possible to compare whether historically the bookmakers have taken more juice on the odds on strongly favoured home teams as opposed to home team underdogs.

Typically a pattern emerges very soon during this iterative process. It obviously makes sense to pursue the most favourable sections. If, for example, less juice is taken on the home teams as opposed to the away teams it makes sense to assess the sections of odds on home teams more precisely. In such a scenario it should be very unlikely that realistically profitable sections would be found on away team odds.

It turns out that if one had placed a bet with Bet365 on the home team of every English Premiership match between 2008/2009 and 2012/2013 from the fifth match day on for which the odds were 2.7 (decimal) or higher the yield would have been 1.6% on the total amount staked on 457 matches. That means that one could have blindly played a number of 457 matches over five years and not only not have lost anything, but one could have made a profit of 1.6% from all those bets. This might not be the margin which fortunes are made of, but the potential which such knowledge holds should be obvious.

One way of utilizing such a pattern of weakness in the odds of bookmakers could be to combine it with one's own system for determining odds, such as a ranking system as described above. Provided one were to stay within this section of the bookmakers' odds one could not only reduce the risk of losses, but practically eliminate the risk of losses. This is a very comfortable situation to be in. The question which obviously arises is whether there could be sections in the range of bookmakers' odds which offer even more value to the better.

The wrong conclusion to draw out of all of this would be to now blindly place bets on English Premiership games in which the odds on the home team exceed 2.7 (decimal). The correct conclusion would be to analyse the bookmakers' odds for popular football leagues in order to identify patterns of weakness.

Every European football league is different. Some are dominated by a handful of clubs, while others consist of very evenly matched clubs. Betting behaviour might differ from country to country. The average better in Spain might behave differently from the average better in England. As the greater volume of betting on a given league is done by the local betting public, as a consequence the patterns in odds for the top Spanish leagues would differ from those in England. Even though every league is different they all have in common that the bookmakers' juice is spread unevenly across the different sections of odds. Knowing and understanding these differences has the potential for "risk free" betting, which is a great place to start from.

Why do bookmakers' odds offer value?

In the previous section the case was made that some sections in the spectrum of odds on European football matches offer better value than others. Historically odds have generally shown a bias towards home teams, resulting in more value in odds on home teams than on away teams. This bias is significant enough to be a supporting pillar of a winning system. In my experience purely relying on the statistical evidence of this bias is comforting, but ultimately not sufficient to put one's uncertainty to rest. A desire remains to understand the fundamental cause of this phenomenon. The remainder of this section is therefore dedicated to some thoughts on possible explanations for it.

In the search for an explanation as to why bookmakers put out odds which show patterns of weakness it is useful to consider the concept of market efficiency. An efficient market is one in which prices are determined correctly on the basis of all the information available to all market participants. What makes the market efficient and therefore guarantees accurate price determination is the information which is available to market participants, and the way in which they behave, based on the information. The assumption is that all available information is priced in at any given time.

Betting volume increases as the event draws nearer. If the betting public were to behave rationally on the information available to them the market should, as a result of increased volume, become more efficient. The relative value or lack of it in the odds would consequently be spread evenly over the complete spectrum of odds on that event.

In European football markets this is proven not to be the case and therefore it cannot be concluded that betters use the information available to them rationally. There must be something at play which causes the betting public to behave in a manner that leads to skewed odds. Another way of expressing this phenomenon is to say that something causes the betting public to make errors with regard to pricing risk.

One possible explanation for this might certainly be heuristics, or flawed intuitive thinking, as discussed above. Jesse Livermore in *How to Trade In Stocks*, offers further possible reasons that also apply to sports betting markets.

> *"All through time, people have basically acted and reacted the same way in the market as a result of: greed, fear, ignorance, and hope. That is why the numerical formations and patterns recur on a constant basis."*

It should be a fair assumption that greed and hope play a substantial role in the behaviour of the wider betting public. A plausible explanation for the home bias could be that betters, even knowing that the odds do not reflect the true probabilities, prefer the lower-probability bet and therefore higher possible returns typically offered on away teams. "If I'm going to place a bet it should be worth it". This results in high-volume betting on the away team. In order for the volume of betting to be balanced there needs to be a shift in the odds to lure betting volume in the direction of a home win. The result is relative value in home win odds. It appears that the opportunities for profitable sports betting come about as a result of deep-rooted behavioural tendencies on the part of the majority of betters.

Choosing a bookmaker

Shopping around for the best odds is critical to successful sports betting. Failing to do so is the surest way to staying a perpetual loser. It is, however, impractical to have an account with a great number of bookmakers. Therefore, one has to identify bookmakers who more frequently offer good odds. These bookmarkers will be the ones that take the least amount of juice. The juice being the difference between the amount the bookmaker takes from betters and the amount it pays out to betters. The amount of juice a bookmaker takes will be determined by the strategy that bookmaker pursues.

Now let us take a look at the underlying strategies that bookmakers pursue. Bookmakers mirror other businesses in that the customer can choose between convenience or a good price. Customers wanting to buy food and other household articles can either go to the convenience stores or to the supermarkets. As a general rule, convenience stores would be located near to where people spend their time. This could be train station buildings or just the high street. It is convenient to shop here, but the prices are likely to be inflated. Supermarkets are, generally speaking, more difficult to reach. However, the prices would likely be lower than at the convenience stores.

Similarly, once in the store convenience comes at a price. Retailers position pricier brand products at a comfortable height on the shelves, so that the customer merely needs to extend the arm. The cheaper articles are placed lower down, so that the customer has to bend down in order to take them off the shelf. To keep things simple, we will therefore focus only on the two strategies bookmakers employ, offering either convenience or a good price (expressed as odds), knowing that there are many shades in between these two general strategies.

	Convenience bookmaker	**Value bookmaker**
Juice	more than 3%	less than 3%
Advertising	Extensive advertising incl. TV	Small advertising budget
Locations	Prime locations and elaborate internet sites	Exclusively internet sites
Experts	Historically extensive teams of experts to determine odds in advance, however increasingly copying odds from value bookmakers	Data analytics focussed team to determine efficient odds and continuously incorporate incoming bets
Typical customer	Masses	Sharps and well-informed betters
Risk management	Extensive risk management teams and processes, betting amount limits imposed on winning customer or accounts closed	Small risk management teams, winning accounts accepted

Betting exchanges do have some advantages over traditional bookmakers. The most obvious advantage is the ability the better has to "lay" results, thereby betting against a particular outcome. Being able to place a bet and to wait for another better to accept that bet is another advantage. Betting exchanges generally share their characteristics with the value bookmaker, as in the table above.

There are two main reasons why a perpetual winning better can only bet with a value bookmaker. The first is that value bookmakers generally offer the best odds and the second is that only (some) value bookmakers accept perpetual winning betters. These two aspects go hand in hand and deserve to be looked at in more detail.

Value bookmakers can be looked at as having developed with the times. They realize that betters are better informed than they have ever been, and that the internet has made shopping for the best odds very easy for betters. Instead of attempting to find enough "sheep" to skim money off, they welcome the sharps. Value betters focus on market making as opposed to determining the true odds with extensive teams of experts. They put out initial odds and then respond very quickly to incoming bets.

Having sharps in their customer base also gives them the opportunity to respond to the bets made by sharps known to them. With this approach they are able to operate with small teams. Even with juice margins of around 2% they are able to operate profitably. Successful betters and, specifically, betting syndicates generally bet far greater amounts of money than other individuals. A margin of around 2% on these amounts can also return a handsome profit. Being transparent and offering value to sharps also ensures that value bookmakers do not have to invest large amounts of money on advertising and lavish appearance, as their customer base is more "loyal" than the masses.

Artificial Intelligence and algorithmic betting

There used to be a time when a sport better could place arbitrage bets by physically going from one bookmaker to the next. An arbitrage bet simply implies that one can place opposing bets on the same market and make money regardless of the outcome. This was the results of substantial differences in the bookmakers' odds. With the advent of computers and, specifically, the internet, markets became more transparent and more efficient. Widespread availability of market-related data, processing capability and transparency are all aspects that lead to more efficient markets. The more efficient a market is the more difficult it becomes to find anomalies in the odds and, hence, value.

In his book *Moneyball*, Michael Lewis argues that the predictions of simple algorithms routinely beat those of well-informed human experts in a wide variety of domains. One of these domains is certainly sports betting. Artificial Intelligence methods like Machine Learning ultimately mean that the amount of data that can be processed and the speed of processing can be increased dramatically. In addition the quality of the processing is also increased. This translates into the bookmaker being able to calculate the probabilities of outcomes even more accurately.

The sophisticated better could also resort to Artificial Intelligence tools as these are now readily available, but this simply means that the mountain to climb for the individual better becomes even higher were he to be profitable. It is conceivable that services will spring up offering betters the service of algorithmic betting. Algorithms will search in real-time for value and place bets accordingly. In stock trading an estimated 70% of all trading is already algorithmic. Trading is done between algorithms in micro-seconds. This section of stock trading is obviously a domain in which humans, apart from programming and maintaining the algorithms, play no active part.

In stock trading there is, however, much left to do for the human investor, and an edge can be achieved, albeit further out on the time horizon. The profitability of the algorithm in micro-seconds does not stand in the way of the human investor making profits in a period of days, weeks or months. This possibility of going out further on the time horizon is much more limited for sports betters.

It should be obvious that Artificial Intelligence will ultimately be leveraged better by the bigger players in the market, the bookmakers. It will make markets more efficient and, as a consequence, leave less value to be had. Altogether it will make profitability harder for the individual better to achieve.

Potential returns

Realistic profit margins

The good news with regard to potential profit margins on sports betting for the better is that the environment has become more favourable in recent years. There are mainly three reasons for this.

- Increased competition amongst bookmakers and innovations like betting exchanges have led to bookmakers reducing their rates of juice and as a result pay out a larger percentage of their takings to bettors.
- Although taxation of sports betting differs greatly from country to country the rate of taxation on sports betting has generally gone down. This is particularly true about countries with a sports betting tradition.
- Greater access to information due to the continuing improvement of services to the bettor on the internet has empowered the aspiring bettor in search of an edge. An examples of such a service is odds comparisons websites which compare odds for any number of bookmakers. It enables the bettor to select the best odds with very little effort.

These factors have not only increased the betters' potential profit per bet, but also increased the number of potentially profitable bets. The two main aspects which determine the potential for profits are the average yield per bet and the number of betting opportunities.

In my experience a profit margin of up to 5% on the total amount staked over a given period of time is achievable. This, however, assumes that the better:

- has a proven system for determining accurate odds
- only makes bets where there is value in the odds
- places bets in the sections of a market where the bookmaker offers favorably skewed odds
- always search for the best available odds
- places a sufficient number of bets (and staying solvent in the process) in order to even out randomness of results

There is no shortcut to profits. Neglect any one of these factors and not only is any profitability impossible, but losses are a sure bet.

Tipping services and "experts"

Betting tipsters come in all shapes. On the one extreme there are sports pundits who consider themselves serious students of their game. This group might include ex-players, managers and sports commentators. It has become a trend for these commentators in print, television or on the internet to announce their "tips" for future events.

The other extreme are those tipsters who offer their services at a cost to the better. Potential customers are lured with the assurance of great profits and preferential treatment with valuable information. The only thing all these services have in common is the fact that they operate at the expense of a rather naïve betting public.

If one is going to wager money on the basis of someone else's advice, should one not at least understand through what process of analysis the person arrived at the recommendation? It is very unlikely that a tipster service would lay bare its method. At best, then, its customer can only ever bet on its recommendations in good faith. For me, using tipster services was never an option, and I would strongly discourage using them.

I did consider tips from respected commentators of their sport for many years. Although many of these commentators mean well there is absolutely no value in their service. I never came across a commentator who offered a plausible explanation for why a particular tip offered value on a statistical basis. Sports forecasting without intensive statistical analysis is entertainment, and not the basis on which to invest hard-earned money. These services are for the gullible masses; stay away from them.

MONEY MANAGEMENT AND RISK MANAGEMENT

Betting bankroll

In motor racing you can have all the engine power in the world, but you need the right set of tyres, or rubber, to transfer that power into speed on the road. In a similar way you could lose your entire bankroll with a great winning formula if you do not have the right money management. For the purpose of this section the assumption is made that you have a winning formula and that all bets are made in adherence to this formula. It goes without saying that this assumption should be your modus operandi if you are to stand any chance of being successful.

The first principle of money management is that you will need a bankroll dedicated exclusively to betting. The direct consequence of this is that this money will not be available for any other purpose. This bankroll should remain untouched for a given time. Let us call it a betting season. Depending on the sport you bet on, this can vary. For football betting I would recommend the full season and, as a more general rule of thumb, one year.

Your betting bankroll will obviously fluctuate. You might be up or down, or both, during a betting season. At no time during the season should you either extract money from the bankroll, nor should you top up the bankroll. Assuming you have a winning formula, you have chosen an appropriate staking plan, as discussed in this section, and you stay disciplined, there should be no need to touch your betting bankroll.

In determining the size of your betting bankroll, never ever include money which you can't afford to lose or set aside for the complete betting season. Greed is a dangerous companion, and so is impatience. Choose a sensible bankroll size. The joy of successful sports betting lies in the certainty of winning, and not in the size of the bets one makes or the speed at which one wins money. Being impatient can be utterly counter-productive. You have to be in the game to win it. Patience and knowing your limits are crucial components of a professional approach to sports betting.

It is very easy to under-estimate how long a losing streak can last, even with a winning formula. I have personally experienced a sequence of 28 consecutive losing bets of which the average true odds were evens (50:50). During such sequences you have to be able to stay within the limits of your betting bankroll.

Bankroll protection and optimal staking

You can only win if you can stay in the game for long enough.

The biggest risk a sports better faces is losing his betting bankroll completely. If the formula employed for selecting bets does not produce an edge for the better over the bookmaker the complete loss of his bankroll is inevitable. A better who employs a winning formula and only selects value bets will make a profit in the long run.

However, even when only value bets are selected it is still possible for a better to lose his bankroll completely.

No one future outcome can be assessed with absolute certainty. Although in the long run a sequence of value bets will return a profit with certainty, in the short run a sequence of value bets can lead to losses. If during such a losing sequence the stake on each bet is too high as a percentage of the bankroll, the better could lose his complete bankroll. The purpose of risk management is to mitigate this risk by employing the right staking strategy.

The purpose is to calculate the optimal size for each stake to ensure that at no point the bankroll is depleted completely. Being overly conservative by choosing very small stakes would obviously guard against a complete loss, but also only ensure small profits. It is therefore a matter of finding a sensible balance between minimizing the risk sufficiently while simultaneously maximizing profits.

The optimal stake size depends on the betters' edge and the average odds of the bookmaker. If the better only bets on low odds where the probability of winning is high (favourites), the likelihood of a long losing sequence is comparatively low. If he only bets on high odds (underdogs) the likelihood is high. Similarly, the bigger the better's edge over the bookmaker the sooner it will become apparent in any sequence of bets.

The second determining aspect for optimal stake size is the staking strategy which is employed. Of the multiple staking strategies available we will focus on the following two:

- Level staking
- Percentage of the current bankroll

A realistic edge over the bookmaker will range, in my experience, between 0 and 5%. Taking this into account a 1 to 2 point (1% to 2% of the bankroll) stake on level staking and 2% on percentage staking offers a good balance between protecting the bankroll against complete loss and meaningful profits. There are distinct differences between the level and percentage staking strategies with regard to the likelihood of a profit for a given sequence of bets. It is therefore required to consider these differences in order to find the strategy which best resembles one's personal preferences.

Level staking is more likely to return a profit over a given number of bets, at the somewhat higher risk of a complete loss of the bankroll. Percentage betting minimizes the threat of complete bankroll loss, but takes longer to return a larger profit. It is therefore a choice between profits after a potentially shorter period, as opposed to less risk and bigger profits after a potentially longer period.

This is due to the fact that, after a losing sequence, the percentage bets are relatively smaller. It therefore takes longer for the losses to be regained. However, over the long run, selecting only value bets would obviously enforce a tendency towards profits as opposed to losses. The better would therefore tend to be up on his original bankroll more often and, therefore, stakes would be higher percentage-wise. Percentage staking should, as a result, return better profits as compared to level staking.

Joseph Buchdahl has done brilliant work on the topic of risk management, and his book *Fixed Odds Sports Betting* is an excellent resource.

Keeping records

Do you know the exact balance of your betting bankroll for the past year? Do you know the exact number of bets you placed and the number of winning and losing bets? Keeping an exact record of all your bets placed and analysing these regularly is critically important. Write down for each bet the most important information. Date and time, the event, your pick, the odds, your estimated odds, the amount and, in short, your reasoning for placing the bet. This will only take a few minutes, and it will have a meaningful influence on your future performance.

Your betting record is the best coach you could possibly ask for. It will tell you exactly whether you are currently up or down. It will tell how you can improve by showing you patterns, good and bad, in your betting behaviour. Take some time at least once a month to analyse your betting record. You will identify patterns in betting behaviour which are not apparent in the day to day routine. It is best to learn from one's past, especially from one's mistakes. Fail to do so and one is assured to repeat these mistakes and pay dearly.

PUTTING IT ALL TOGETHER

Sound principles

Very few sports bettors ever make a profit over the long term. I wrote this book in order to tell you that it is possible to gain an edge over the bookmaker. As I tried to demonstrate you will however have to change your approach in order to do so. Only through an analytical approach and by following sound principles in a systematic way can you stand any chance of becoming and staying profitable at sports betting. The bookmaker always follows precisely this analytical and systematic approach and leaves nothing to chance. Only your best game, only such a professional approach can reap positive results.

The following synopsis of the main principles that have been discussed should serve as a checklist. Come back to it as often as possible until every one of these points has become second nature to you.

1. Approach betting as investing

Successful sports betting will never be achieved by hoping for positive results. Success can only be achieved if one develops certainty that one has a systematic approach which over the long term will yield positive results. This is a change in mindset towards a more analytical approach and the patience which comes with certainty. The effect of this change in mindset will be profound on your approach and results.

2. Set aside a betting bankroll

A betting bankroll is the money that is allocated for betting purposes. For a whole range of reasons this money should be kept separate from that which is required for everyday expenses. If your bankroll gets depleted or you are having to top it up this is a clear sign that sports betting might not be for you.

3. Only bet singles and on sports events with a league format

Single bets on an individual event offer superior value as compared to multiples and perms. Stated more clearly, there is no value to be found in multiples betting. Equally, live sports betting, that is betting during the event is a losing proposition. It is purely instinctive in nature and does not lend itself to analytical analysis. In addition the bookmakers juice on live betting is such that value betting in a systematic manner is practically impossible. Sports with a league format offer the prerequisite for success as far as data and the possibility for analysis is concerned. These vital attributes are absent in tournament sports.

4. Specialize

There is no substitute for developing an edge if you are to be a long term profitable bettor. The only way to develop such an edge is through specialization. Identify a sport and a market and strive to become the ultimate expert in it by using the best available data and most thoughtful analysis.

5. Develop a system for determining odds

The bookmakers odds simply reflect the probabilities of the outcomes of an event. It is a price which reflects risk and reward. The only way to know whether a price is worth taking is to have an own estimate of what the price should be. One therefore needs a system which is proven to provide accurate estimates. This system should be based on the analysis of historical data. It should be tested in order to validate the accuracy of its results and be updated continuously with current data.

6. Only place value bets

Trying to pick winners is a fools game and can never lead to long term profitability. A dealer of any kind of merchandize can only make a profit if he pays less for the merchandize than he can sell it for. This is obvious. The same principles applies to sports betting. The only way a sports bettor can make a profit is by only placing bets when the bookmakers odds are more favorable to the bettor than they should be.

7. Identify market segments with minimum risk

The bookmakers odds for certain segments of a market will offer more value than others. This is due amongst other things to the bias of the betting pubic. Recreational bettors want to make a quick buck and in order to do so are prone to backing the underdog in order to capture the higher odds. The bookmaker would have to respond and move the odds in order to balance its risk. This creates value on wins for home teams. Systematically analyzing markets and finding these favorable segments can greatly reduce risk and enhance potential profits.

8. Compare bookmakers odds

In the age of the internet there simply is no excuse for not searching for the best odds before placing a bet. Small differences in the odds over time add up to big differences in the outcome.

9. Size bets sensibly

Even with an edge over the bookmaker a losing streak can continue for a much longer sequence than what logic would suggest. Whether your strategy is level or percentage staking as a rule of thumb one bet should never exceed two percent of your bankroll. You have to stay in the game in order to win.

10. Manage your emotions

It is impossible to be a successful sports bettor and enjoy the thrill of being emotionally involved in bets at the same time. If you give into the lure of looking for the trill, you will be a loser. The biggest thrill of all is the one of losing when the stakes are high. The brain is after the hormonal rush. How the rush comes about is not relevant on this level. If you do not have your guard up you will end up high on emotion and low on money. This might be the single biggest pitfall to your success. Stay well clear of this pitfall by never watching or otherwise following an event live on which you have placed a bet.

11. Keep betting records and analyze these regularly

No other activity will yield more benefit per unit of time invested than keeping and analyzing records of your betting. With only a few moments required to document each trade and half an hour analysis a month you will always know exactly where you stand in terms of your performance. In addition you will discover patterns in your betting behavior, good and bad, that will otherwise go undetected.

12. Accept losses and stick to your system

Never chase after losses, meaning to let the next bet be influenced by the previous loss. Accept the loss, there is never a sure thing. As stated above trying to pick winners is a fools game. Successful betting is the result of a sequence of value bets. If this is clearly understood the bettor should be more at peace with losing a value bet than with winning a bet which lacked value. This is the mindset of the investor. Knowing that the system employed is sound. The result is certainty that the current loss is merely one event in a long term winning sequence.

THOUGHTS ON FREEDOM

In the pyramid of human aspirations, freedom ranks right at the top. Although freedom has many possible dimensions, the ability to be financially secure and to be able to engage in activities of one's choice is a universal aspiration. I believe that a longing for this type of freedom is the core motivation for the majority of sports betters. Yes, many get caught up in the excitement and emotional rollercoaster that accompanies risk taking. Still, I believe that most merely look for a way to get at money doing something enjoyable, as opposed to a job which might be unsatisfying. If the assumption is correct that the wish for freedom is a main motivation for sports betters, then we have to assess for whom this might be a realistic wish. And for whom it is not.

As a knowledgeable sports better you are faced with a crucial decision. You can use the available knowledge to find a winning formula. This is a process which involves much dedication and discipline. It should have become clear from previous chapters that the odds are stacked against you. Not only are you up against an industry which has for generations skimmed almost every better, but the government also does its part to make successful sports betting nearly impossible through taxation.

You can also use the knowledge which is now available to you to come to the recognition that it is best to walk away from sports betting. If financial freedom is the goal, one in a hundred will achieve this through successful sports betting. The other ninety-nine per cent will in fact sacrifice freedom as a result of sports betting.

The following questions, if answered honestly, should help you discern which pathway will bring you closer to freedom.

- Do I have a solid understanding of statistical methods and am I able to apply these skills on historical data using a computer program?
- Do I have a minimum of ten hours a week to invest in developing and maintaining a system to determine odds for the markets I intend to bet on?
- Am I comfortable with never following an event live that I have placed a bet on?
- Am I comfortable not placing a bet for a period of six months while I work on perfecting my system?

If you are one of the very few who can answer all of these questions with "yes", I would encourage you to proceed with vigour and hard work. You have the basic pre-requisites to become profitable at sports betting. If the answer to any one of these questions should be "no", I would encourage you to stop betting immediately, permanently!

This chapter was written some seven years after the core of this book was completed. During this time I have further explored the concepts discussed in this book and each and every one of them has been validated. I have also stopped betting on sports altogether, although I maintain a keen interest in sport betting markets. Why did I stop? Once I had started making profits systematically I had entered into the ranks of those who systematically take money from the masses. I had been given privileged circumstances and knowledge to develop an edge. I was now using this edge to take money off betters who were not equally well equipped. This didn't feel right to me.

Still, it took time, and I had to overcome much inner resistance before I could let go. I had worked very hard to develop a winning formula, and to relinquish benefiting from it was difficult. I recall the walk in the woods during which I decided that I would stop. Unexpectedly, from that moment on I felt wonderful, relieved, and I have never looked back in regret once.

The title of this book is *Freedom Through Sports Betting.* That is, how I found freedom through sports betting. It was not the financial freedom I had set out to find, but inner freedom. Since then I have gone on to another field of investing altogether. Here I am up against big institutions and the smartest people out there. My opposite number now is fair game, and I revel in making my pickings as the underdog. Not to profit from sports betting was my subjective decision. If you are the one in a hundred who can systematically make profits, go for it! If you are not that one, having read this far you are now fair game in terms of having your money systematically taken from you.

Not everybody is destined to compete in the finals of the hundred metre sprint at the Olympic Games. Not everybody is destined to make money at sports betting. Fortunately, there are a multitude of disciplines to compete in. For you this might be something completely different. It might be a craft, a service you perform or a job you really enjoy.

The Greek philosopher Thucydides is quoted as having said, "The secret to happiness is freedom... And the secret to freedom is courage." Be courageous and make the changes, difficult as they might be, that will set you on your way to freedom.

Bibliography

Books

Kahneman, Daniel (2011), *Thinking Fast and Slow,* Farrar, Straus and Giroux

Anthony, Robert (1991), *Betting on Yourself,* Berkley Books

Livermore, Jesse (1940), *How to Trade In Stocks,* Duell, Sloan & Pearce

Buchdahl, Joseph (2003), *Fixed Odds Sports Betting,* High Stakes Publishing

Allen, James (1903), *As a Man Thinketh,* St. Martin's Publishing Group

Papers

Malkiel, Burton G.; **Fama**, Eugene F. (1970). "Efficient capital markets: a review of theory and empirical work". The Journal of Finance. 25 (2): 383–417.

Cain, Michael, **Law** David, **Peel**, David. "The Favourite-Longshot Bias and Market Efficiency in UK Football Betting". Scottish Journal of Political Economy

Websites

http://www.football-data.co.uk
https://www.bethelp.com
https://www.winnerodds.com

Printed in Great Britain
by Amazon

46655966R00047